LEARN ABOUT PLANTS!

Seeds

By
Steffi Cavell-Clarke

KidHaven
PUBLISHING

581.46
CAV

Published in 2018 by
KidHaven Publishing, an Imprint of Greenhaven Publishing, LLC
353 3rd Avenue
Suite 255
New York, NY 10010

Designer: Danielle Jones
Editor: Charlie Ogden

Cataloging-in-Publication Data

Names: Cavell-Clarke, Steffi.
Title: Seeds / Steffi Cavell-Clarke.
Description: New York : KidHaven Publishing, 2018. | Series: Learn about plants! | Includes index.
Identifiers: ISBN 9781534522442 (pbk.) | ISBN 9781534522404 (library bound) | ISBN 9781534522329 (6 pack)
| ISBN 9781534522367 (ebook)
Subjects: LCSH: Seeds–Juvenile literature. | Plant anatomy–Juvenile literature.
Classification: LCC QK661.C38 2018 | DDC 581.4'67–dc23

Printed in the United States of America

CPSIA compliance information: Batch #BS17KL: For further information contact Greenhaven Publishing LLC, New York, New York at 1-844-317-7404.

Please visit our website, www.greenhavenpublishing.com. For a free color catalog of all our
high-quality books, call toll free 1-844-317-7404 or fax 1-844-317-7405.

PHOTO CREDITS

CONTENTS

Page 4	What Is a Plant?
Page 6	What Is a Seed?
Page 8	What Do Seeds Look Like?
Page 10	Where Do Seeds Come From?
Page 12	Seeds on the Move
Page 16	What Do Seeds Need?
Page 18	How Do Seeds Grow?
Page 20	Seeds in the Greenhouse
Page 22	Tasty Seeds
Page 24	Glossary and Index

Add Sunshine

Words that look like **this** can be found in the glossary on page 24.

What Is a Plant?

A plant is a living thing. All living things need water, air, and **sunlight** to live.

There are many different kinds of plants. Most plants have roots, leaves, flowers, and a stem.

Plants live all around the world!

5

What Is a Seed?

A seed is made by a fully grown plant.
A plant typically makes a lot of seeds.

A seed can grow into a new plant. It needs water, warmth, and sunlight to grow.

7

What Do Seeds Look Like?

poppy seeds

sunflower seeds

coconut seed

Seeds come in many different shapes and sizes. All seeds can grow into plants.

A seed often has a hard shell, which protects it until it is ready to grow.

Horse chestnut seeds have spiky shells!

9

Where Do Seeds Come From?

Seeds can also grow inside fruit, such as apples.

A seed generally comes from a plant's flowers.

The center of a sunflower is made up of many tiny flowers that all produce seeds.

Apple seed

Seeds on the Move

Seeds generally move away from the plant that they grew in. This gives them the best chance of survival.

Some seeds are blown away by the wind and become buried in soil.

A dandelion flower uses the wind to move its seeds.

13

Some seeds grow inside fruit or berries. When birds eat fruit or berries, they eat the seeds, too.

14

The bird will then fly away, and the seeds come out as waste somewhere else!

The seeds will still be able to grow!

What Do Seeds Need?

Most seeds need to be buried in soil to grow. They also need water and sunlight.

Once the seed has everything it needs, its hard shell will split open, and a new plant will begin to grow.

17

How Do **Seeds** Grow?

As the seed splits open, roots begin to grow downward and a tiny shoot begins to grow upward.

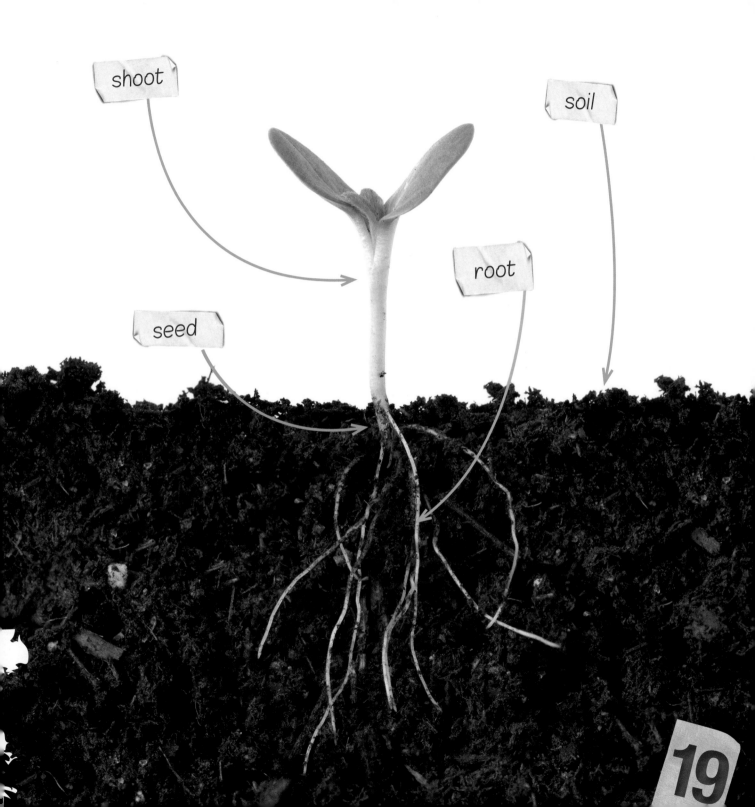

shoot

soil

root

seed

19

Seeds in the Greenhouse

A greenhouse is a glass building where people can grow their own plants. Greenhouses can stay warm even in cold weather.

Many different types of seeds can be planted in a greenhouse and kept warm.

A gardener waters the seeds to help them grow.

Tasty Seeds

Did you know that baked beans are seeds?

There are many different types of seeds that humans can eat. Many of these seeds can be eaten as a healthy snack!

Peas are seeds that come out of their own little pod.

pea pod

23

GLOSSARY

grow	to naturally develop and increase in size
protects	looks after and keeps safe
soil	the upper layer of the earth where plants grow
sunlight	light from the sun
survival	the ability to stay alive

INDEX

birds 14–15

flowers 5, 10–11, 13

fruit 10, 14

roots 5, 18–19

shells 9, 17

shoots 18, 19

sunlight 4, 7, 16

warmth 7, 20–21

water 4, 7, 16, 21

wind 13